# Etchings 34.2

Literary and Fine Arts Magazine of the
University of Indianapolis
Winter 2022



Etchings
literary and fine arts magazine

1400 E. Hanna Ave.
Indianapolis, IN 46227



Cover Design by Etchings Staff
Cover Art by Sydney Pinkstaff
Printed by IngramSpark

etchings.uindy.edu

# Editorial Staff

# Table of Contents

# Letter from the Staff

Letter from the Editors,

To begin, we would like to thank everyone who has played a part in making this volume a work of art—from our submitters, judges, advisors, fellow editors, and launch party attendees. With all of your love and support we are able to continue to publish pieces by UIndy students, staff, and alumni. In particular, we would like to extend a huge thank you to this semester's Dorlis Gott Armentrout Award judge Joyelle McSweeney, who is a writer and professor at the University of Notre Dame, for volunteering her valuable time to review the accepted works. Also, we are grateful for the advisorship of Professor Kevin McKelvey and his continued support of *Etchings Literary and Fine Arts Magazine* alongside our English Department and Shaheen College of Arts and Sciences.

We hope you enjoy this curated reading experience as contributors delve deep into topics of motherhood, grief, love, retrospection, and more. As *Etchings* continues to progress with our ever-evolving world, we want to remind readers that many pieces are written for mature audiences, so please take note of the content warnings on select works to avoid undesired distress. Furthermore, we strive to accept pieces from diverse perspectives and backgrounds in order to support our UIndy family and foster a community eager to learn about the lives of those around us. Likewise, we hope you take this opportunity to appreciate the art of others with respect and empathy.

Before you dive into the magazine, we'd like to quickly draw your attention to an important formatting feature. As previously explained, some of these works contain themes and language suited towards mature audiences, and could possibly be triggering. Please read these works with caution. They are labeled with a content warning (CW) including a brief description of said content, and are marked by a thin yellow bar on the side of the page.

With love and gratitude,

*Etchings* Volume 34.2 Staff

# Dorlis Gott Armentrout Awards

**Winner:** "Easier Than Teaching" by Mackenzie Hyatt (p. 44)

**Runner-Up:** "You" by Destini Mink (p. 70)

**Honorable Mention:** "I Read Deborah Miranda During Church" by Jonathan Thang (p. 16)

# Dorlis Gott Armentrout Judge

## Joyelle McSweeney

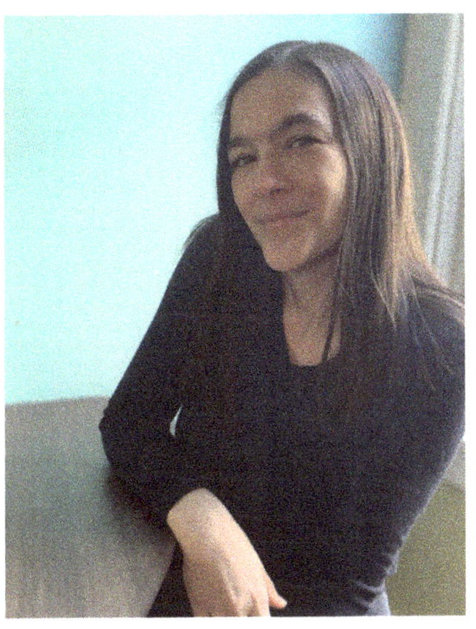

As a poet, prose writer, playwright, critic, and publisher, Joyelle McSweeney is interested in the ways in which writing moves among genres, languages, media, and materials. She is the author of ten books, most recently the double poetry collection *Toxicon and Arachne* (Nightboat Books, 2020), called "frightening and brilliant" by Dan Chiasson in the *New Yorker*; *The Necropastoral: Poetry, Media, Occults* (University of Michigan Poets on Poetry series, 2015), a book of goth eco-criticism; and the verse play *Dead Youth, or, the Leaks*, which won the inaugural Leslie Scalapino Prize for Innovative Women Playwrights. With Johannes Göransson, McSweeney founded and edits Action Books, an international press for poetry and translation. She lives in the Rust Belt and teaches at Notre Dame.

# Joyelle McSweeney Interview

**Etchings:** How long have you been writing?

**Joyelle McSweeney:** I'm one of those nerds who's always been writing! I can remember my first poem, which I wrote in second grade, in soft pencil on that cheap newsprint with the dotted lines your teacher gives you to practice your letters: "Tiffany is my friend / until the end." Not a great work of genius, but maybe just a tiny bit sinister! Look out, Tiffany!

**Etchings:** What is your writing routine?

**Joyelle McSweeney:** An important part of my writing routine is 1) coffee and 2) reading. Reading other writers' work lets me move more securely into that part of my brain where my own writing appears. Or maybe, encountering other folks' art (be it music, painting, fashion, dance) softens me up to where I can receive the messages the universe is sending me!

**Etchings:** What is your approach to working in multiple genres?

**Joyelle McSweeney:** Sound leads me. I follow the sound where it wants to go. Sometimes that's a prosey sound, long sentences with pools of assonance, sometimes it's spiky, phrasal, and lyric. No matter what genre I write in, I follow the urgency of sound.

**Etchings:** What's one piece of advice you would give a prospective writer?

**Joyelle McSweeney:** Geek out. Make a little shrine in your mind—or maybe literally, on your desk!—of your favorite things, the things that make your heart leap and your brain buzz. It could be the music that plays as your fave game loads, some vintage commercial you remember playing when you watched TV at your grandma's house on summer nights, some nickname you always felt ambivalent about, an earworm that follows you around. Let all this music and noise and cacophony and language flow into your writing; it's a soundprint of where you've come from, and where you're going; it carries the voices that have shaped you, for better or for worse, but it's also uniquely your own.

# 2021 Whirling Prize Winner: Poetry

## TAK Erzinger

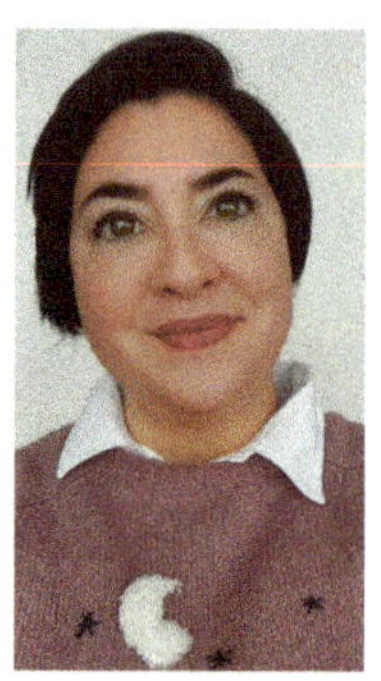

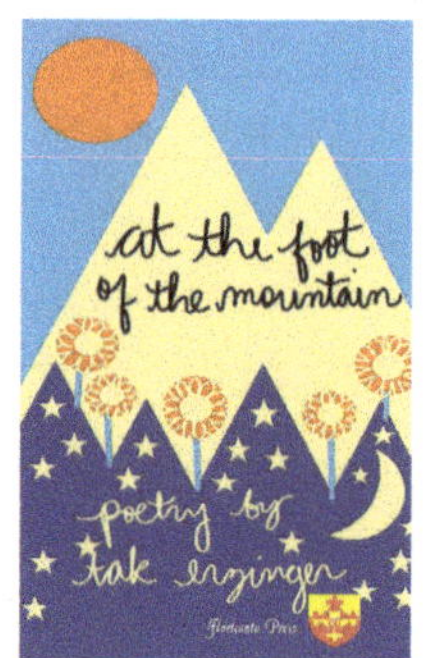


**TAK Erzinger** is an American/Swiss poet and artist with a Colombian background. She is also an alumni of Boston University and an English teacher. Her poetry has been featured in Bien Acompañada, The Muse, River and South Review, Welter, The Rational Creature, and more. Erzinger's illustrations/art have been featured at or are forthcoming in *Latina Magazine*, T*he American Visionary Art Museum*, Ponder Savant, and more. Her current poetry collection "At the Foot of the Mountain" was published by Floricanto Press out of California, 2021. She lives in a Swiss valley with her husband and cats.

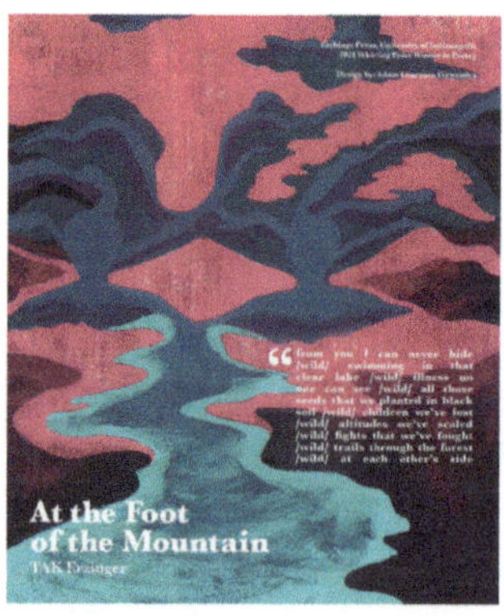

# 2021 Whirling Prize Winner: Prose

## Richard Louv

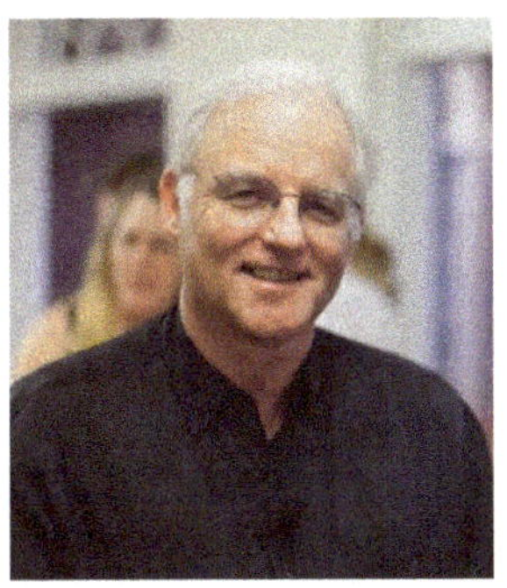

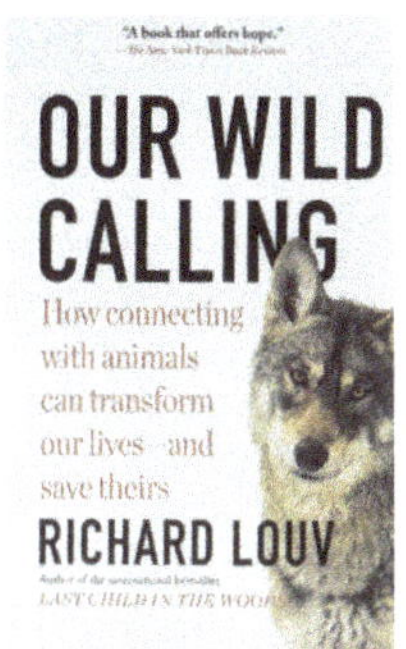


**Richard Louv** is a journalist and author of ten books, including *Our Wild Calling: How Connecting With Animals Can Transform Our Lives - And Save Theirs, Last Child in the Woods: Saving Our Children from Nature-Deficit Disorder*; *The Nature Principle*; and *Vitamin N*. Translated into 21 languages, his books have helped launch an international movement to connect children, their families, and communities to nature.

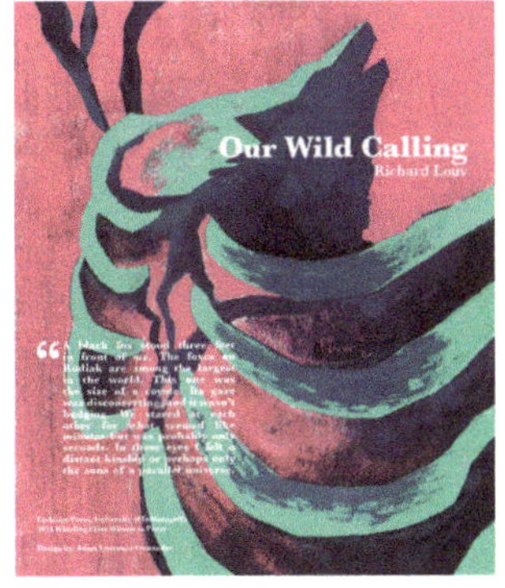

# Seeing the Beauty in the Little Things

Elizabeth Dubak

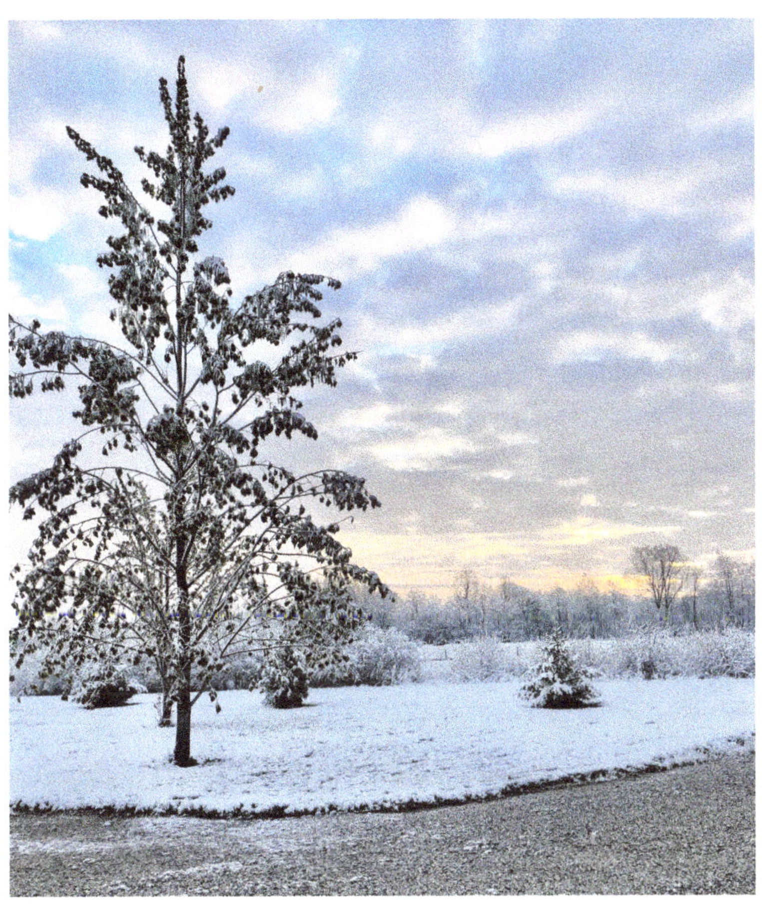

# I Read Deborah Miranda During Church

Jonathan Thang

I read Deborah Miranda's *Bad Indians* during church, and I stormed out four times. I got angry several times... listening to the pastor dressed in a grey suit and matching pants speaking in Falam about God and the Bible. The first time I stormed out was during the part where they were praying and welcoming a new member to the congregation—a baby, a baby born a few months ago. It could barely open its eyes and had already been chosen to place its faith in and devote its life to Jesus of Nazareth. It was at this moment that I was finished with the introduction and got to the first section of the book: the story of the mission Indians and the pastors. The baby wasn't crying; it was asleep, I think. It must've been asleep because it would've cried if it were awake from the sound of my self-righteous and indignant shoes stomping the carpet floor as if it were guilty of all of the feelings festering within me. And it was.

The second time I walked out was when the pastor was beginning his sermon. I don't remember what it was about, but I did see a few nods in the crowd in front of me, so it must've been something they agreed with. At this point, I had reached the section about flails, whips, and cudgels. I don't want to talk about what I was thinking here. How could they not see it? I googled the history of the Chin people. Apparently, we practiced animism. I asked my mother about it, and she only replied, "Oh, I didn't know."

It was a ceremony back in the country to baptize children months after they're born. My mother was one of these children, and so was I. But who do I have to blame for this? The British? They were the ones who colonized us and made us adopt their English alphabet and their religion. But now, as I gaze over the crowd of devout Chins who are listening intently to the words of the pastor, who is making them do this? Over half of the words the pastor spouts are either borrowed from English or descended from English words. If I were to blame the Brits for this, then that'd mean they have the power to force people to not come up with new words on their own. And I'd rather not give them this amount of power.

I was angry. Angry at how they have the audacity to not be angry. How can they sit so quietly in a church that represents the people who took their life from them? Miranda was angry, so I was angry. I had every bit of right to be as angry as she was. I didn't know about all of the atrocities that the white men unleashed on my ancestors in the way she did, but I could still see the effects—but I was still angry. It was here that I realized that these people that I called my people weren't my people at all, merely imposters. Of course, they looked and sounded and acted and dressed like my people, but they weren't. If they were, they wouldn't be sitting next to me in this church—this damn church. It was big and new, and they bought it three years ago for a few hundred thousand dollars. Did the British make them buy this building with a connector hallway and a full-sized gym? Maybe. But the British didn't force them to be so happy to go along with it.

They're imposters[1].

I asked my mother what the Falam word for elbow was a while back. I had forgotten the word once before and she's told it to me before. I'd always forget the Falam words whenever I speak, and it'd always be at the most embarrassing times. This time, I was talking to a friend—a white friend—who was asking me Chin words for everyday stuff, and he arrived at the elbow. I paused for a second. I tried to ruminate deep in my

1 sus

thoughts for anything that resembled "elbow" in my native tongue, but nothing would come up, not even at the tip. I don't remember what answer I gave him if any. If only he'd asked me about anything else… he would've been more knowledgeable and I would've never had to ask my mother. Of course, Miranda had to ask questions as well. It's normal.

I met another Burmese student at school during my second semester. She asked me where I was from (which region or city) and just generally tried to get to know me better. It was a weird experience. She started by speaking to me in Burmese and when I told her that I didn't know how to speak Burmese, she looked at me with a look I'd ever only reserved for other people—other Chin people, that is. I explained to her that I was Chin and that I'd forgotten how to speak Burmese after years of not using it in the U.S. Her look died down a bit, and of course, it did. After joking about how the only Burmese I knew was "ထမင်းစားပြီးပြီလား," she let me off the hook. She even asked me to join the club for Burmese students. I gave her my number to register me for the club. I never attended any meetings.

It's not that I didn't care for the club or being Burmese. It's just that how can you expect me to be a part of a group with "Burmese" in the title while not being able to speak Burmese? They spoke English, but I was sure some way or another that their native tongue would slip out for the sole purpose of embarrassing me. That thought got me riled up but not enough for a justified rant. The ability to speak a language does not denote a person's ethnicity is what I told myself when I decided to ignore that first text from the club. The sting decreased with every subsequent club meet. I never did attend any meetings.

My mother asked me to explain to her how to use the word "however" in a sentence. I responded in a garbled mess of

English and Falam, trying my damnedest to explain to her the English grammar while speaking English in a Burmese accent with sprinkles of Falam here and there in a dimly veiled attempt to sound like I was speaking to her in our native tongue. She didn't ask me to repeat myself or explain it differently, and she didn't need to. Her look told me everything. I turned to the sink to scrub the dishes and faintly told her to go ask my sister.

I read Miranda during church. The sermon was still rambling incoherent nonsense mixed with legible English words. I gave up trying to listen to the weekly sermon years ago. I complained about his usage of English, but at least I could understand it. I could never make out half of what was spoken in Falam. Worse was when they'd use Burmese words for words that Falam didn't have, or even worse, other dialects of Chin. My mother was born in a Mizo household, but she is fluent in Falam because that's what my dad's family spoke. I've thought about asking her to teach me certain phrases and words in Mizo, but I could never find the words to say it in Falam.

The sermon was almost over. My mother slapped my hand, waking me from my existentialist ideologies and the tiny AirPods hidden behind my disheveled hair. She signaled me to go ahead outside to pick up my brother from Sunday School. I waited for about ten minutes before they were let out. He grabbed my hand and pulled me onto the gym floor to play and spin him around until the sermon was finished and we could all go home. He didn't speak a lick of Falam so he asked in the little broken English that he could muster. I spun him around, and he fell flat on his stomach, laughing. The sermon was over, and mom came over to pick us up to go home. Later that day, I wrote my reading response for the book. I don't remember what I wrote about. I just remember reading it during church.

# Indigo

## Mia Lehmkuhl

oh, little one
it seemed just yesterday you were cast unto my arms
to the embrace of one just as clueless
as you discovered this world set before us

the antics of children once chilled my spine
twitching and squirming at the very thought
that one would end up mine

but i saw my purpose laid out in front of me
to give you not the role of sister
but the role of pseudo-mother
mimicking the tricks of the trade

so i carried you through the mountains and through the valleys
nourishing you with only my love and hope
of a better tomorrow
where i'd make it only long enough to watch you stand on your
own
without me having to clutch your hand

for my fingers are frostbitten from keeping yours forever nimble
and these arms of mine have grown tired from barbed thorns
i embedded them just under my skin
so she didn't prick you, too

you see, behind the baby wraps and warm milk bottles
my back was bloodied from the lashings of her tongue
and only when you slept against my beating heart
did i release my sorrow into baby blue blankets

every day that passes that you are not returned to my arms
remember i am watching you graduate from muddy creeks
 and training wheels
you're a big boy now
with scraped elbows and shoulders to hold the backpack that
 will be your armor until you grow big and strong

eat your vegetables
so you don't need me anymore
i'll always sit criss-cross applesauce in your memories with
 action figures in hand
begging to play pretend one last time

to hear the chirps of your laughter
and the leftover relics of my innocence in your voice
in a burst of melancholy tears
i feel enough youth for the both of us

and as i say goodbye until the next season
my heart is filled
with the bittersweet pride
of the sister who mothered you at fourteen.

# Held at Birth

Adam Fernandes

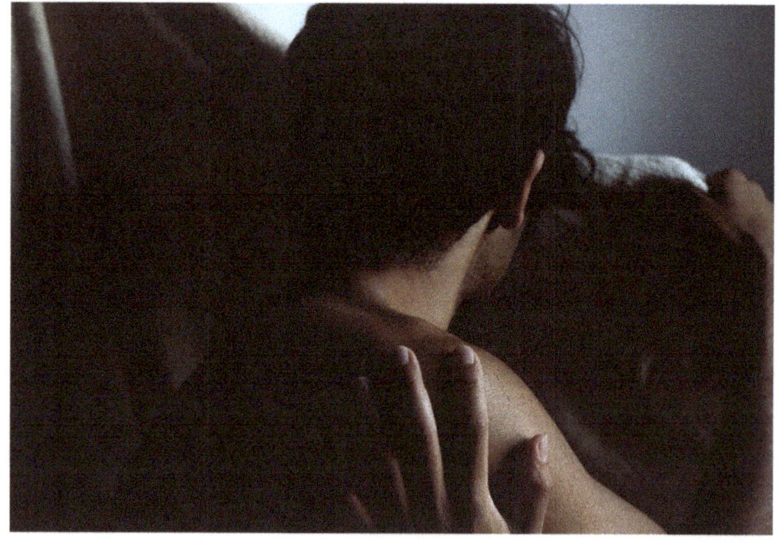

# Father Kunze

Alec Cizak

*CW: graphic imagery*

A tiny black bird,
pale, rim-shot eyes
slammed into a pane.

Father Kunze
brought the corpse
to the table,
bobbling the creature's
broken neck
like a light switch.

He passed it left,
asked us to ponder
the fragility of life

as we ate breakfast,
and fondled a dead bird
with our bare hands.

# Mama

Alec Cizak

They say I'll shout Mama
the moment before I die,
that I'll forget they ripped me
from your womb as you
surfed an epidural slumber.

You never cradled me in
your teenaged arms before
they handed me over to
the people I call Mom and Dad,
the ones who wiped my ass,
changed my diapers, and wept
when they learned I filled
my heart's hollow chambers
with a different kind of
chemical snooze.

I still wonder who you are,
              where you are,
                            if  you are.

Will my search cease
as they dim the lights, my
last gasp on this brutal stage?

I know your name.
I do not know your face,
your breath, your touch.

I imagine cold fingers
that grim moment, the final act,
draping a dirt quilt over cobalt eyes
you armed me with, shutting off
the spotlight, hushing an audience
you chose not to be a part of.

# Biter

## Olivia Cameron

*CW: graphic imagery*

*Something is horrifically wrong with my daughter*, I realize as I look out the kitchen window. Even though I'd always know—deep down in my womb since the beginning—the thought still rocks me. I set the knife down, abandon the carrot I'm chopping for a seat at the table. My head flurries with future possibilities and plans, but I keep ending up at the beginning.

-

He's sitting on the couch with the stick in his hand. It's so white, the lines so pink against his tan palm that for a moment I allow myself to believe it's not real. I wrap my arms around myself, bracing for the blow. The inevitable explosion that I dread but can't—won't—run from.

"I don't know how," I say when the silence goes on too long. "I'd been so good with the pills."

He didn't look up. His shoulders rose and dropped with a low sigh.

"I'm sorry! I'm sorry I hid it, I'm sorry you found it. I'm sorry!" I squeak out, tears breaking through.

And then he was on his feet. My first reaction was to fall to the ground, protect my head from whatever might be thrown my way, but before I could make it to the floor his arms were around me.

"I'm so happy. I'm going to be a dad." He squeezed me. It didn't hurt, but I was more afraid than ever.

"I love you. We're going to have a baby!"

Even though I'd already made the abortion appointment, I said nothing. Because for one moment, I had everything.

-

The virgin mother herself wouldn't have been treated better during her pregnancy. That is, if people had known she was carrying the son of God. I might as well have been.

I was sick the entire nine months. I threw up constantly and violently. Every time it felt like I was fighting against something, or someone. Like the baby was testing me, seeing how far I was willing to go, how much I could take before I called Planned Parenthood again.

But the growing fear of the small being in my body was covered up by the love I was being showered with. He took me on dates again. He bought me flowers every week and always came home on time. Not once in those first thirteen or so weeks did he yell or curse at me. Even when I puked on the carpet or burned his dinner because I was too busy bent over the toilet to take it out of the oven.

When he was there he would hold my hair back while I emptied everything in my body—except the real sickness—into the toilet. He would put me in the bath, turn the warm water on and let me soak while he cleaned the bathroom. It reminded me of my mother. When I was little, anytime I threw up she would place me in the bath and get her spray bottles and sponges from the cabinet under the sink. This reminder of childhood was enough to make me think that he could be a good dad. If I kept being good, kept being pregnant, he could love me. Love us. He wouldn't leave again.

My mother once told me that I was prone to delusions.

-

There was so much blood. I was certain I was dying. I cried and screamed at the nurses holding my hands and legs, and at the doctor sitting between them, trying his best to deliver the demon that was ripping me apart.

"We're almost there. Your baby is okay."

I hadn't asked about the baby.

But then she was there. Not just an abstract thought or a flutter in my stomach. Living, screaming, crying. When they put her on my chest, I didn't dare whisper those words that parents love. *Don't cry, baby.* I knew better. She had every reason to cry, and so did I.

It wasn't love at first sight. In my body I felt a great splitting—two continents coming apart, their edges becoming puzzle pieces. Mother and child. I would never just be me again. I would belong to her until I died.

There was resentment, at first. I had given up all I had left—my selfhood—for this being that destroyed my body, that I didn't even want. And where was he? Where was the father as I laid there, bare and broken?

Next, there was the guilt, which accompanied the affection like a close friend. I looked at the helpless little thing and knew that it wasn't her fault. I had done this to myself, to her. I allowed her to be born into this shitty world so I could revel in my fantasy just a little bit longer.

As she put her mouth to my breast and suckled life from me, I decided to spend the rest of my days making it up to her.

Then: "Ow!" There was a sharp pain on my nipple. I looked down, my eyebrows knit in confusion. The nurses had turned to look, ready to offer their advice and help to me, the new mother. I pulled her away from my chest. As she opened her mouth wide to cry, I noticed two tiny teeth, covered in my blood.

-

Years later, on a Tuesday afternoon, I picked her up from preschool. I was helping her pack her things into the tiny princess backpack she'd chosen on a Target trip when I noticed her teacher hovering around us.

"May I speak to you for a moment?" she asked once she caught my eye.

I nodded and told the little girl to continue packing up and say goodbye to her classmates. As I followed the woman to a corner of the room, away from the children, anxieties raced through my head. Was she a troublemaker? Showing signs of a learning disability? Exhibiting symptoms of a contagious disease?

I noticed the teacher picking at her long red nails. "We are having a bit of a *biting* problem," she said with a shy smile.

"Biting?" I asked. I could feel cold sweat forming on my neck and suddenly my hands were cold. Memories of morning sickness arose. I knew my physical reaction was a bit dramatic—kids will be kids—but this was my kid. My little monster. "Like...other kids?"

"No, but..." she replied. "I'd been noticing marks on her hand occasionally. Obviously from a child's teeth. I even saw her biting her hand during play time, but I remembered you saying that she can be a bit anxious, so I figured it was just a nervous habit. Like biting your nails."

Of course I already knew this. It was an innocent habit of hers, always in response to any kind of attention or being in a crowded place. It was just one of those things that made her who she was.

The teacher cleared her throat. "Today I saw her bite so hard that blood ran down her arm. I was shocked, I ran to her with paper towels and cleaned her up. I thought she would be crying. She was...completely fine. Actually, happier than I've ever seen her."

I swallowed. "That's disturbing."

She nodded.

"I can, um, talk to her about it." I wasn't sure what to say.

While we walked to the car, holding hands, I rubbed my thumb over the bandage on my daughter's tiny hand.

-

Elementary school came around and I still couldn't get her to stop. I tried everything. I put mittens on her hands but she would just take them off as soon as I wasn't looking. I made her use hand sanitizer, but the taste didn't deter her. I even took her to a child psychologist, who told me nothing and wanted a couple hundred dollars an hour to take an unknown amount of time to get answers.

I had to accept that this was what she did. She was the little girl who loved to bite herself hard enough to draw blood. I was the mother of this little girl. What had I expected from the baby born with teeth? Admittedly, my own child freaked me out. She had since the beginning. But she was mine.

I kept my promise of retributions for the life I'd given her. I defended her to every teacher who complained and every parent who didn't want her around their kids. *Biter*, they called her. *Fucking little vampire*, the other moms whispered to each other on field trips.

Still, somehow she managed to have two friends from the neighborhood. Two little girls from next door, sisters just a year apart that were homeschooled. I was glad that she had friends. The absence of friends combined with a biting issue could mess her up for life. I also feared the accusations of neglect and bad parenting that she might use to blame me one day.

They were playing in the backyard one spring day. I was watching from the patio and decided to get them some juice as it was unseasonably warm. I tried to be quick, knowing how little kids love to get hurt as soon as you turn your back on them. But when I emerged from the sliding door with cups of grape Kool-Aid, what I saw was worse than a scraped knee or bee sting.

The little girls stood in a triangle formation. My daughter was the point at the top, her right arm extended to her younger friend and her finger in the small girl's mouth. The younger friend did the same, her finger in her older sister's mouth. And then that friend's finger was in my daughter's mouth.

And then they all bit down. Blood ran down my daughter's lips as her friend started wailing. I was frozen, watching the odd scene unfold.

"You said it was a pretend vampire game!" The girl screamed, clutching her hand close.

My daughter didn't say anything, just smiled and licked her lips. The little sister jumped on her, little fists flying to avenge her sibling. I ran to put a stop to the madness, but by the time I got there it was too late.

My kid had bitten the small girl's cheek, tearing off flesh.

That was the last time she saw her friends.

-

I shake the memories out of my head. I resume chopping, and finish making dinner. When everything is finished and food is on the table, I call her in from the living room.

Her bite marks multiplied like rabbits over time. Any place on her body she could reach, she started biting from. They're getting better, though. At least she doesn't do it to herself anymore.

I sit next to her and start eating. There's no movement except for my own hand shoveling forkfuls into my mouth. I give it a few minutes, wait for her to take a bite of something she's supposed to. She doesn't. She has a sour look on her face.

"What is it?" I ask her.

"I don't want this." She pushes her plate away, pouts with her little lips.

I sigh. Not wanting to have this fight, I ask her another question. "What *do* you want then?"

A little smile breaks across her face.

"Fine."

She crawls into my lap and sinks her teeth into my neck. I count the bite marks on my own body to pass the time. When I get lost after fifty, I stop and look up at the ceiling.

"This is the last time," I lied.

# Nemesis

Alrielle Viewegh

I sizzle
With a fire built in my bones.
It burns
And courses through my veins,
Igniting a fiery rage.
Thoughts tear through me,
    *I'm a windstorm threatening to surge.*
Teeth gnash in an
    Inexplicable rhythm.
I ponder
    Wonder
Choose to believe that
There is more than one side
Of me.

*My skin will drip off of me*
*As if it's been dipped in acid.*

*Avenge your desecrated body,*
*They chanted.*

Tear me apart—
Then build me up
    *renewed.*
I know that I may be a temptress,
But your Fate is surely
    Doomed.

# Red Eyes

## Cambel Castle

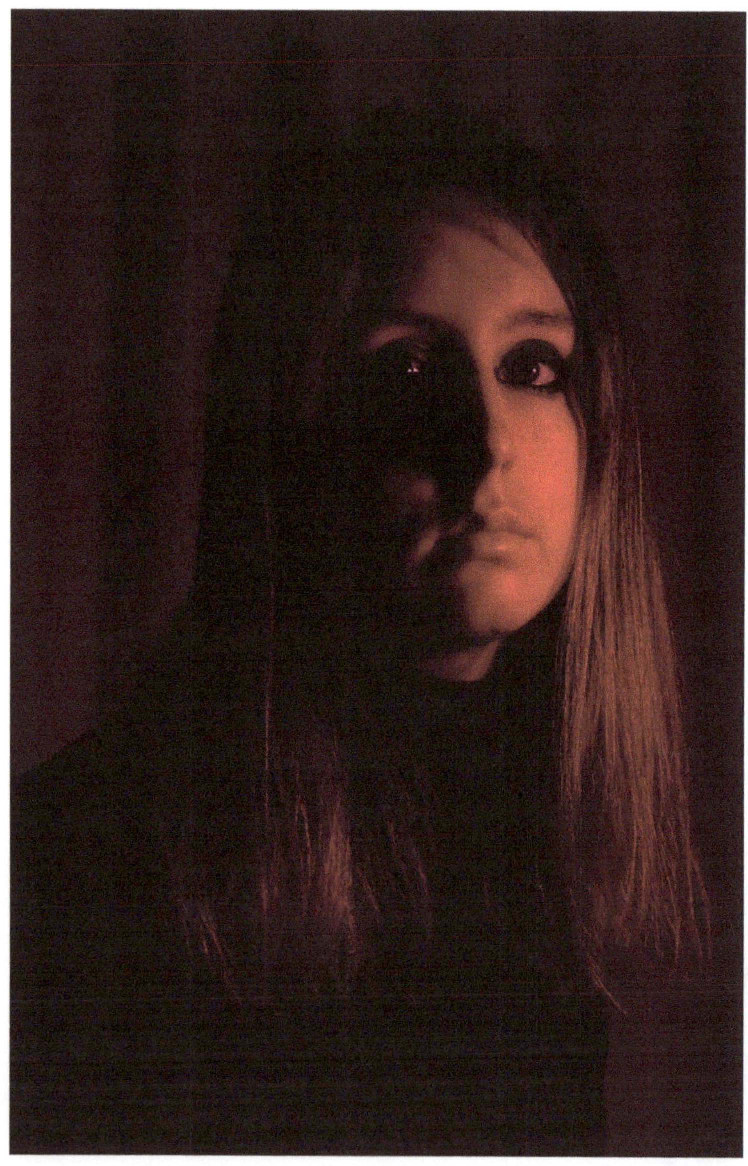

# The Color Red

Cambel Castle

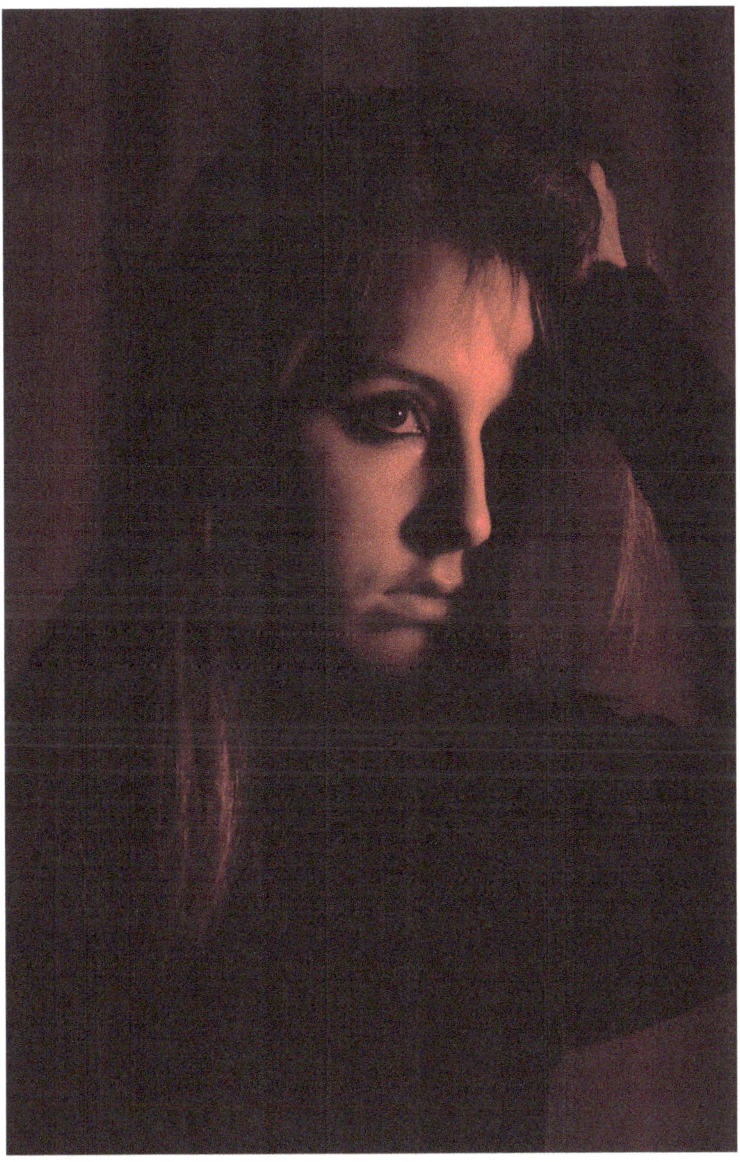

# Red

## Cassi Dillon

The weather was my favorite kind
Wind rushing through your car
On the back roads
My hair ricocheting off of
The half-opened window

My hair was as red as the blood
Flowing out of my heart
And into your hands

But there is a gaping hole in my chest
That you left there
And I had never felt so vacant

Your greedy hands reaching for more
While my hands were empty

You always liked my hair black

Less passionate, less vibrant
        *Angry.*
                *Red.*

More like the dirt
That filled up my lungs
When you were around
        *Dead.*
                *Buried.*

In the palm of your hands
Lay the blood in my veins

Every fractured piece of me

That you had set flames to
Red.
Red.
Red.

# Drowning the Flame

## Sierra Durbin

Her hair resembles the fiery embers of a conflagration's miraculous appearance—bold, beautiful, and brilliant. The tips spark while wind from the brewing storm blows beneath the ashy, weeping clouds. A menacing growl escapes from the forming mist, intimidating the dauntless blaze. Droplets trail from the sky, extinguishing the fearsome flames. Water rises like a creeping spider crawling closer up her skin. She grows smaller as transparent walls restrict her to a confining box, filling with water. She struggles to fight against the current, an anchor of worry weighing her down. After splashing frantically, she senses water approaching her lips. Ice-cold water fills her lungs as she gasps for breath, her mouth dry and bitter from the salt. Aggressive, midnight blue waves threaten to engulf her spirit. The water becomes a suffocating blanket. Her thoughts compete in a relentless race; however, time remains her enemy. To survive, she must combat self-doubt. Sinking beneath the water, the frail creature glimpses at the horrid sea monsters patiently waiting, mouths open and full of razor-sharp needles. Her heart pounds out of her chest. A pungent smell of smoke lingers in the air. She endures a roller coaster of terror and nausea. A shrill squeal fills her ears; her body feels numb. Weakness is strength: she keeps pushing forward. Suddenly, the calm melody of a whale song echoes in her ears. Hope sparkles in the distance with the sight of land. Her cheeks flush like a rose with the returning flame, and she recalls that no matter the obstacle to always keep swimming.

# Infection

## Kaitlyn McCoy

Sometimes I wish that I would sew my own mouth shut.

The guilt of the things I say without thinking keeps me up
so often alone in the dark that I wonder if I am truly a
bad person
Simply masquerading as someone good.
I have convinced myself that all I want is to be
Nice — helpful — kind — selfless —
And yet I am afraid my true nature peeks out around the façade
at those moments
When my mouth blurts out something my mind did not think.

I hate my mouth — myself — when I say without thinking
And the guilt and shame overpowers any good feeling I've
ever had
And then it's all that I think about;
My failures,
Moments ago;
And years ago I remember
Conversations long forgotten by everyone else except me,
where I hate myself for things that only I remember.
It haunts me like a ghost — a specter I can't quite get away from
Only I can see it
Everyone else has forgotten, has moved on, has forgiven —
*(why? I don't know)*
— But it still is gripping me at the throat with a long, clawed,
dirty hand

And though it hurts I *want* it to hurt, I *want* it to take my air
and my voice and make sure I never utter another word.

I want someone to shut me up — forcefully, violently, with the taste
of blood in my mouth.
Sew my mouth shut —
Cut out my tongue —
Rip my throat out —
Or take away my voice —
I do not care.
But make me have penance for the little things I've done and said
Because though they are small — the little things add up to
large things
And I do not wish to hurt anyone else any further.

# Reflection

Cambel Castle

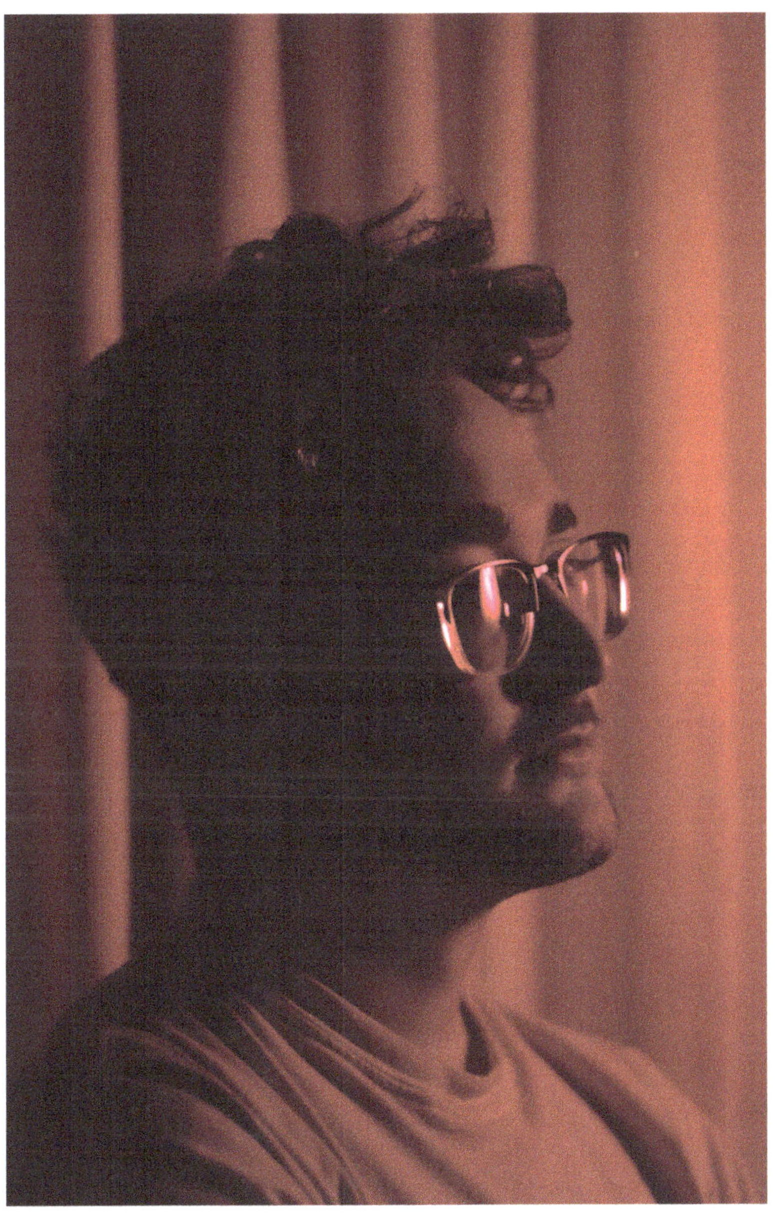

# The Horror Within Us

## Emma Knaack

*CW: self-harm*

What's the most painful way you can imagine you would be capable of killing yourself? For me, it's skinning myself alive. Don't try and deny it. Saying you don't know what you would do. Everyone does.

I know some of you out there will come up with much more cliché answers. Maybe you'd shoot yourself? Overdose? Hang yourself? Cut your throat? Not me. I want people to stare. To know me as I am now and then to watch as my body slowly disintegrates. I want to show people how ugly a thing death is. It's something you can't look away from, but wince at its unpleasant sight all the same.

Each day, I will walk out of my house with a new body part in mind. Knife in tow, I will start to play my skin like a violin. Passersby will wonder if I'm a street performer. I set my hat before them with examples of tips inside. Knives. Scissors. Razor blades. A few people will watch my act. Wincing at the sight, but unable to look away. Maybe I'll have a fellow lunatic or two tip me with new instruments. Are they now accomplices to my death? I personally won't hold it against them.

The knife eases its way into my skin. The blood peaks through, scared of what I am planning to do. My fingernails sink into myself, brown blood stains hiding under them from the day before. Once I have my grip, I peel back the freshly sliced layer. Again. And again. And again. It will get to a point where my skin is so thin you can see right through it. In that moment, those watching will know I'm alive. Will know that what they are watching is death.

Each day I execute my show. Each day I collect more accomplices and bystanders to my death. That way, when I do finally die, everyone will remember. Even those who didn't watch it firsthand. Stories will get out, videos will be shared, and eyewitness accounts will be told. Those who watched me will have to live with that. And don't let them fool you into thinking they "didn't know what I was doing." They knew. Why else would they watch? They always knew. Remember, this death is against my will. I don't want to kill myself, but in this hypothetical I've created, circumstances force me to. And if I must go before I have made my mark on this world, I will do the next best thing and leave a trail of blood to my grave.

# Easier Than Teaching

Mackenzie Hyatt

*CW: references to sexual assault*

Whistle, wolf, and starve,
because a step-crushing snow may interrupt
the response you're hungry for,
strain your ears for a scream in response.

Bugle, elk, still in velvet,
let steam spill from your mouth in the cold,
swear that you don't feel a thing
and pick fights with all the wrong monsters,
swear that you will never be a trophy.

Cry, killdeer, wing askew,
limp
and lure lovely coyote,
make her pity you until the others are out of sight.
Say she saw a meal in you.

I am sorry, deer, I am sorry that I cannot tell you
why they scar you, why they scar each other.
They say it is in their nature, but—
here, take your knife and your pepper spray—
this is easier than teaching killdeer not to lie.

# Two Paths Split in the Woods, and I Died

Ethan Thurston

I went for a walk
On a cold night
Lit by stars and Moon
I heard your voice call out
And my heart grew with excite
You must have decided to join me
I came closer to your call
My feet skipped along the ground to the tune of your voice
Your emerald eyes like treasure through the trees
As you pulled me to the sky
Your embrace warming my skin
Our faces grew close and your warmth
Gave my body life
I couldn't move
I didn't want to
How could I choose to leave perfection
I give you the love I have left
As it spills red upon the forest floor
My only hope
Is that none of it goes to waste

# The Whale & The Waltz (2)

Adam Fernandes

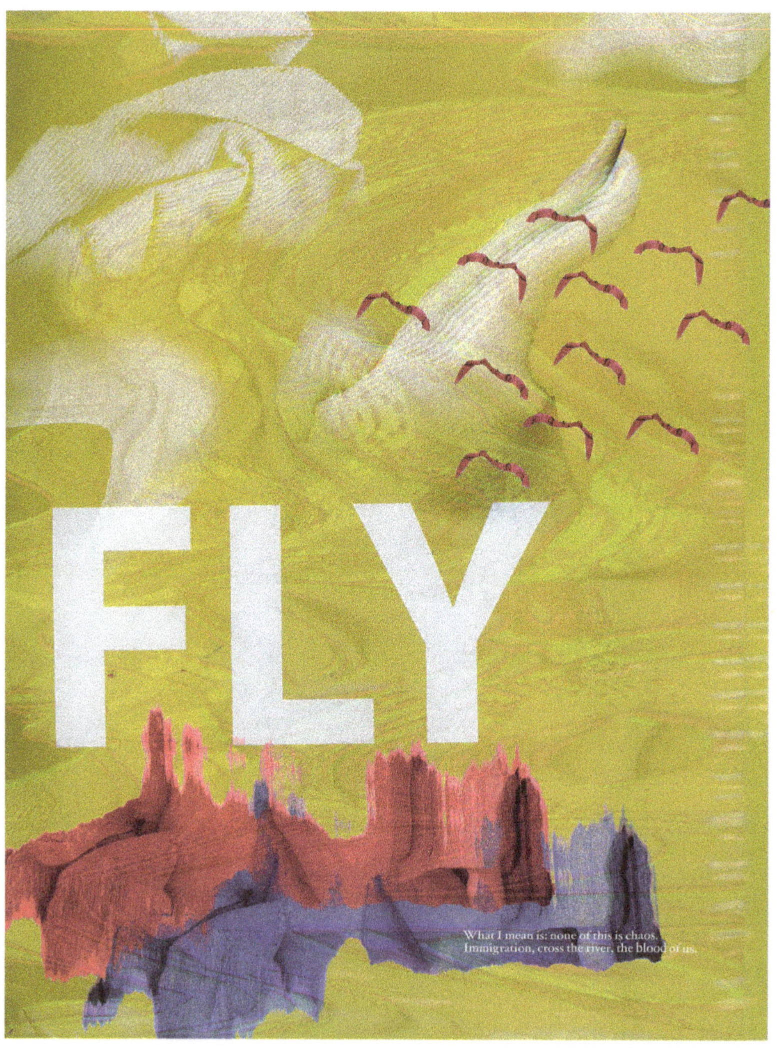

# The Whale & The Waltz (3)

Adam Fernandes

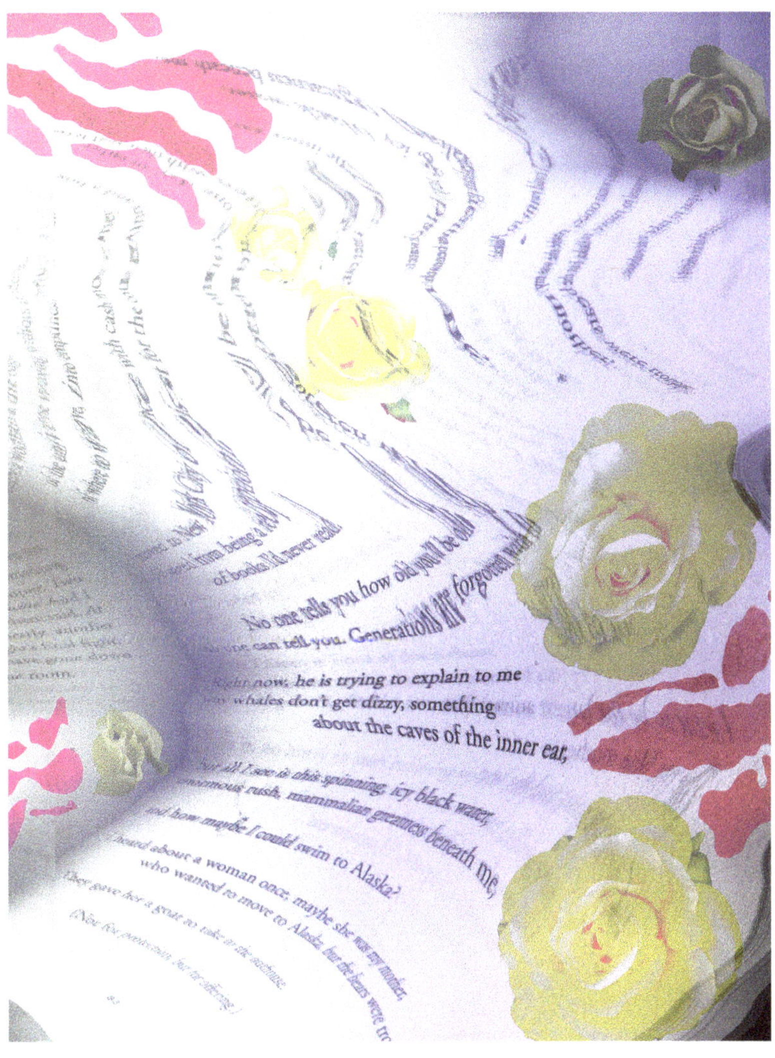

# The Swing

## Olivia Cameron

Once, when I was a little girl, I came upon another child in the woods. She was sitting on my tree swing, the one my father built for me. It was situated just by my favorite lake. If I swung myself high enough in the air, I could feel the adrenaline of being above water—the possibility of jumping—making my heart pound. But I never would. I was quite afraid of dying. Her long blonde hair was whipping up, down and around as she kicked her legs and pulsed through the air.

"Who are you?" I asked with a mastered girly bluntness.

"Who's asking?" she retorted.

I ignored the slight. She was on my swing, after all. But I wasn't in the mood to argue. I'd already done that this morning with my mother, and I was now dreary from using all my energy to antagonize her.

"That's my swing," I stated simply. "I came to use it. I don't have much time."

She seemed to ponder this.

"So I'd like to swing now."

Her eyes, which I can't quite remember the color of, rested on me with disinterest and slight annoyance. It reminded me of my mother when I'd ask her to play. It reminded me of the morning.

"Okay." She jumped off easily onto the forest floor.

I waited for a moment, expecting her to collect herself and go home. Instead, she stood and watched me as I sat on the wooden board and wrapped my hands around rough rope.

Suddenly, she turned to the water. "Can you swim?" She asked.

"Yes," I said. "Well, I'm not great at it. But I can do it." I didn't know why I was telling her this. She had done nothing but steal my swing and annoy me. Now, I realize, it was something about her face. When I imagine it, I see my reflection in the lake water, the reflection I used to stare at for hours on end, thinking about my face and being alive and other various abstract thoughts.

"I can. Very well. I could teach you."

Becoming very bored with her swimming talk, I started swinging. "No. Thank you."

"I want to play with you," she said. Her voice was pleading, and almost forceful. She was looking right at me, her eyes following me up and down as I went.

I thought about this for a moment. I felt bad for her, but I really wanted to be alone.

I decided that it wouldn't kill me to be nice. "You could push me!" I exclaimed in the air. I pretended to be excited, so that maybe she wouldn't ask to be pushed instead.

What happened next is hazy. She didn't say anything else—at least, nothing that I heard—as she came behind me to push.

Her small hands pushed hard, hurting me a little bit each time, but it wasn't enough to complain.

I remember closing my eyes and breathing in the air. I liked to do this, picturing each smell in my mind. I liked to apply colors. That day, the woods smelled like green, brown, and burgundy.

In the time I had my eyes closed, trying to and successfully recalling the word "burgundy," she had pushed me higher above the water than I had ever been. When I looked down at my feet, all I saw was murky and flowing green.

"Too high!" I yelled.

She pushed harder when I came down.

"Too high!" I reiterated.

Hands digging, pressuring my back.

"Stop it!" I screamed. I don't know why I didn't jump off as soon as I came back down. I suppose I was too scared to think straight. But sometimes I wonder if it was because I didn't want my mother to get mad at me for getting dirty, for there was no way to jump off at this speed without falling in the dirt.

Also, I hoped that this stranger would just stop. When I'd played with other children, it was normal for them to be naughty, to try to push buttons, but they never went too far. Nobody ever got seriously hurt.

When that last push came—I honestly don't know what happened. Maybe she pushed extra hard, scooting me to the edge of the seat somehow. Maybe I had decided to jump, but waited too long to act. I can't be sure. I am sure, though, that by the time I realized I was falling through the air I hit water. I'm uncertain of the angle, but I'll never forget the cold rushing over my head. It was like icicles had been driven into my eardrums with a pick.

Looking back, the water could not have been very deep. But I've never gone back to find out. And I've had plenty of time.

You see, I did emerge from those waters. It took a lot of kicking and grabbing, but I pulled myself out. I dragged my body on the land, mud and rocks rubbing against my belly, long hair darkened by wetness falling in my face. My lungs and nostrils burned even though the rest of me was ice.

Once I had composed myself, I looked around for the other little girl. She was gone. And in a childish desperation for vengeance, I went searching for her. I trekked through the forest for hours, then weeks, then years, which turned into decades. Over time my hair has fallen out in long strings. My teeth have rotted into nothingness. My skin has peeled and dropped off of me like the rind of an orange. Eventually, even my clothes were eaten away by moths as they fell from my bones.

I walked and walked until I eventually came back to my swing. A girl was there. Long blonde hair shimmered in the sunlight. I walked over to her, expecting she would scream at the sight of me. Instead, she gazed with curiosity and disdain for my arrival.

"Who are you?" she asked.

I looked into the water, trying to figure it out myself. I still looked like me. But I knew: I was no longer a little girl.

"Want a push?" I asked her.

# Bee Happy

Sydney Smith

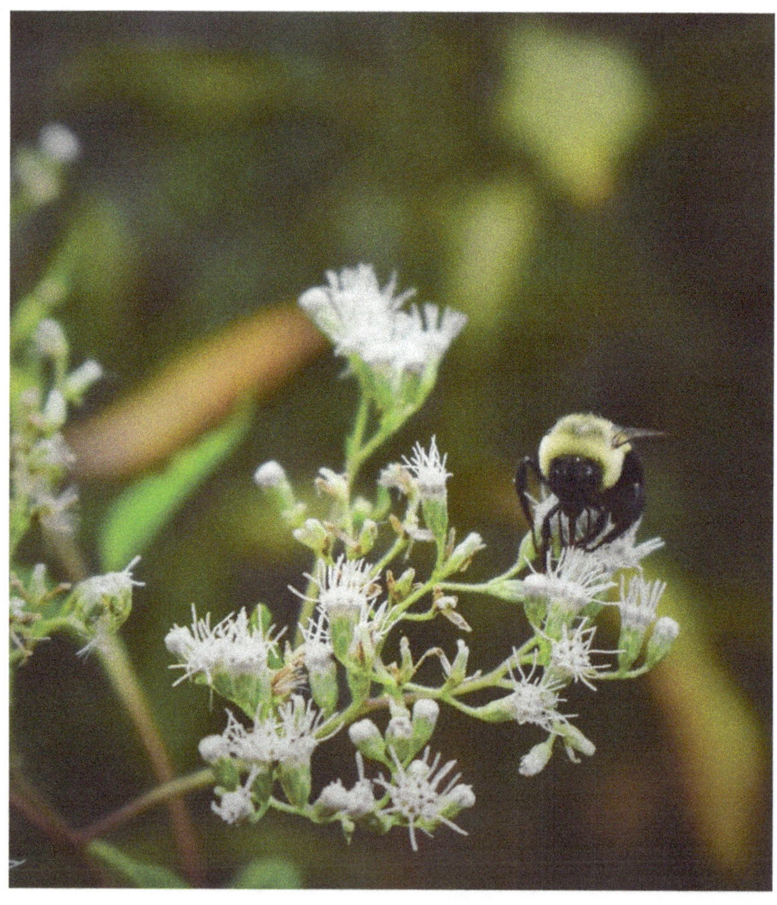

# Awakening

Sam Jackson

The freedom is bittersweet today,
as the full force of my being comes out
to stretch its legs and breathe
sighs of relief.

In spite of your delusion, and my
desperate complications, I want you to know
I finally feel free to find confidence in a
mind and body that can be both delicately powerful
and indominantly reserved.

Not all the pieces have come together, and
although my odyssey is far from completion, it's
a different kind of bracing to find some new peace
in what I previously failed to believe in.

From here on out, I'll assert myself, and
I'm daring you to understand something outside
of what you know, this is what it feels like to be
unchained and world weary, the least you could do
is wish me luck in this new life on the edge of certainty.

# Silver Blossom

Sydney Pinkstaff

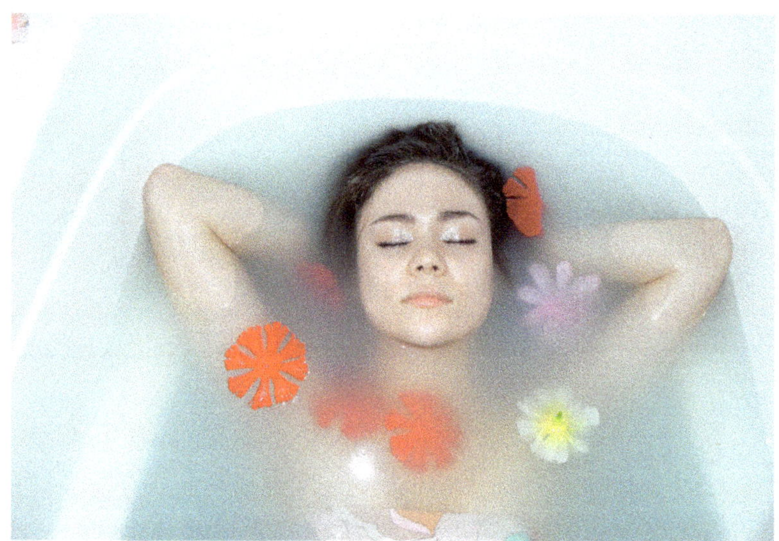

# Countdown

Breanna Emmett

What is the metric to measure the progress of a healing heart?

Is there something that can tell you when it is safe
to be you again, something to gauge the distance
between you and the next resurrection?

Slip a stick past your blue lips, under your stiff tongue,
let it soak in the ash and iron dusting the flesh
of your gums. Wait for it to analyze

every frozen and forgotten cell in your bloodstream,
to taste the carrion within, and spit out a date in return:
*Five days. Ten days. A month.*

*A year.* However far away the day may be, mark it down
on a calendar pinned to the wall across from your bed
so you may shine a spotlight onto it. Stare

as X's appear under the drag of the pen, and wait for your heart
  to beat again.

# An Apple a Day

## Olivia Cameron

Fiona Apple taught me
how to be a woman.

took me into her orchard,
cut herself open,
right down the middle,
with a sharp, sticky knife.

she fed me her seeds,
popped them in my mouth
one by one.
striking a key
pianoing down my
esophagus
landing in
my stomach.

she must have soaked them in kerosene,
because they stoked that
fire in my belly.
the fire i extinguished
over and over again,
for years and years,
until her voice hit my ears
for the first time.

Fiona Apple taught me
how to be an apple pie.

slice yourself into pieces,
serve yourself up with
vanilla ice cream and
a warm smile
as you watch them choke
on the very seeds
that gave you fire.

# The Whale & The Waltz (1)

Adam Fernandes

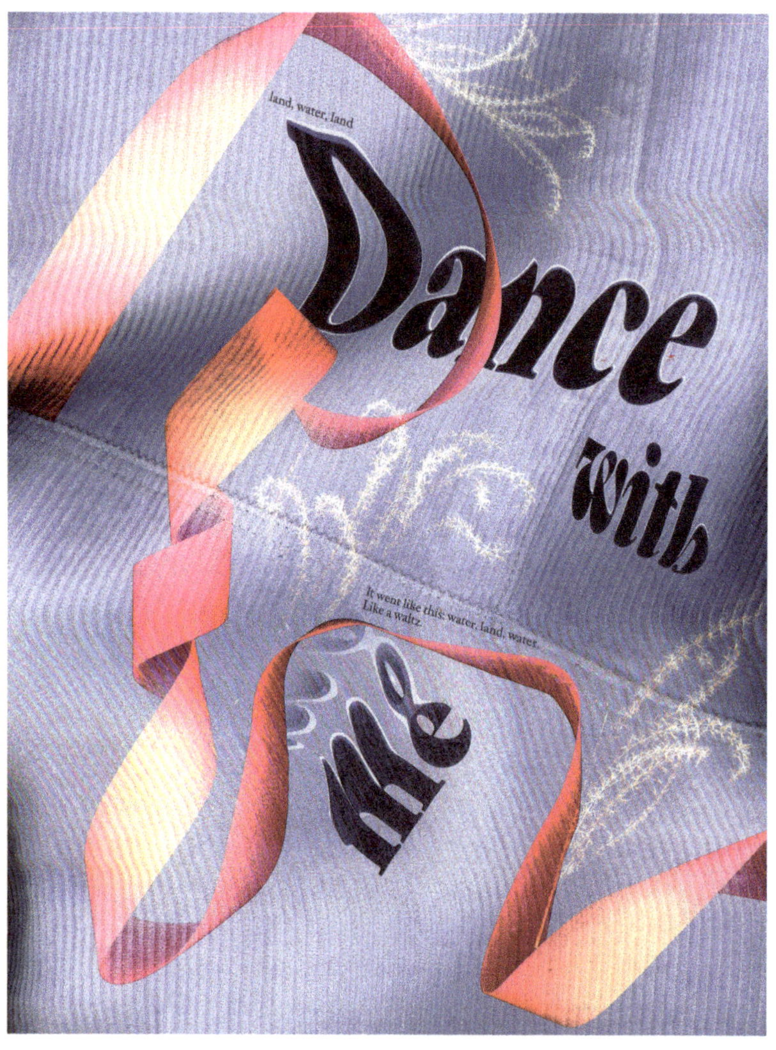

# Dead End

## Jordan Dashiell

Taking personality quizzes on Buzzfeed
While your best friend masturbates in the bathroom
You don't know who you are or what you want to be
So on Thursdays you ask old men in online chat rooms

Stripper heels and your ex's shit leather jacket
Walking down to the Speedway you used to work in
You can't afford the discounts in yellow brackets
So you love the manager when nobody's lookin

Kraft Mac 'n' Cheese
Wine stains on the couch
Dirty dishes in the sink
Coke in a purple pouch
Torn hair and sheets
Your landlord calls you a slouch

You were the queen of prom
And now you live in a slum
Your dresser's full of needles
Cabinet's full of rum
Your sister calls you a slut
Your father calls you a bum

# Cherry

## Cassi Dillon

You said I was sweet
Like candy
Dripping from your lips

Cold hands gripping your shoulders
Warm lips latched on my neck

You made me feel beautiful

You said I was sweet
Like sugar
In your favorite lollipop

Cherry flavored
Always licking your lips
Greedy for the taste
Of me on your tongue

You said I taste like sin
But you were too busy
Basking in my body
Like I was your goddess
To care if you went to hell

You said you didn't need air
If it was me
You were breathing in

Teeth sunk in my skin
Soft
        Soft
                Soft

You miss my cherry taste
On your flavorless tongue

# Recreational Beating

## Cassi Dillon

I opened the door in a too big sweater and leggings. You only commented once on how I always wore pajamas. We first met on Christmas Eve, I think it symbolized everything you were going to be to me. A gift of some sort. We didn't talk about how we were both alone. I always enjoyed your company. We laid there and you called me pretty. I didn't think I would hear from you again after that first night. I was shocked that I did, to be honest. Seeing my phone light up with your name always made me happy. I remember all of our plans, all of our shoulds and woulds. We never made it that far but I wish we did.

You always complimented me, it made me feel so comfortable. A kind of comfort no one before you gave me. A kind of comfort I haven't had since. You told me you liked my body and my first instinct was to not believe you. But why would you lie? If you didn't like it you wouldn't have kept coming back. Right? Nonetheless, I wondered what the other women you were with looked like. If they were skinnier, if they had bigger butts, if they looked like me. My insecurities rang out every time you touched me. I wanted to crawl out of the same skin you caressed so carefully. I didn't think anyone could ever be as tender with me as you were. I picked myself apart and you glued it all back together.

You gave me your shirt once, I told you it wasn't going to fit, that my breasts were too big. You didn't miss a beat, "That's the point." I know you just didn't want me to feel insecure. You were really good at that. You once gave me a long monologue about how beautiful bigger bodies were. I was in awe watching you talk about it. You were so convincing, I almost believed you. My size is something that has always made me insecure, but it didn't faze you one bit. You showed me it wasn't the end of the world, and that maybe I have more to offer. You found me beautiful, something I still find hard to do myself.

I kept you to myself like stolen whispers in between the sheets at the most vulnerable hours. Much like we did all of the time. I miss our nights staying up talking. I remember the rain hitting my window as we delved into our deepest feelings. You told me things I haven't forgotten. I wanted to know you, and I never want to forget you. Even though you might forget me. I didn't have the same impact on you as you did on me. We never tried to be anything we weren't. I didn't stand out from the other women. I never tried to. I knew what we were, I never tried to kid myself into believing it was anything more.

You held my face as you told me you didn't want a relationship, not specifically with me; just in general. You had been hurt before and you didn't think it was worth it. We were on the same page there. You get close to people just to get disappointed. I was never a steady place to land anyway, I'm always running. I can't take the heat, so I run before it touches me. I think you said it so I knew that we would never be more than a night kept between the sheets. But I didn't need a reminder.

I remember our last times together. You started texting me more. I wore a dress for you. We were walking down the hallway and you couldn't stop looking at me.

"What?" I asked, feeling insecure.

You smiled and shook your head, "Just mesmerized."

You told me I was beautiful, and when I didn't know how to react you told me it was adorable. You held me tight into your chest as you said it, like looking me in the eye was too vulnerable. As if you looking me in the eyes would solidify it for you, and neither of us were ready for that.

I miss our late nights, almost dying in your car on rainy nights. Laying on your chest and listening to you breathe. I miss your hands in my hair and your lips on my neck. I still feel the remains of you in the middle of the night.

My bed is empty of your warmth, and your arms are empty of me.

I wonder if we could have ended differently, or if we were doomed from the start. Maybe my insecurities were too loud for me to let you love me entirely. Maybe it was me, as it always seems to be. Maybe I felt the flames too close to my skin and ran without looking.

Or maybe it was you. Maybe you lit the match. Maybe it was your plan all along.

I guess I'll never know.

# Desire

Adam Fernandes

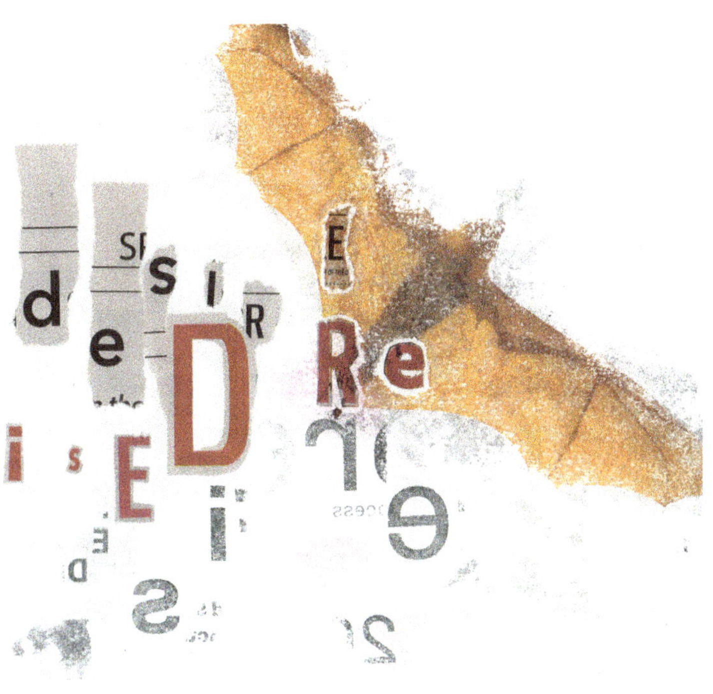

# 5 Centimeters Per Second

## Shyam Patel

*-Inspired by the movie "5 Centimeters per Second"*

Heavy feet travel great distances
as our hearts are hidden away
within rooms of sorrow,
I have locked myself in from the start.
If tears flow freely in whispering wind,
like fall blossoms,
will this tenderness return with sweltering heat?
If fall blossoms fall
5 centimeters per second,
how long might it take me, too,
to fall to the ground so gracefully?

# Nothing (Shower Song)

Jordan Dashiell

Cash register dance while I tally up my minutes
Dump those silver hours onto her teeth
Déjà vu, I'm living out my same past month
In separate installments of the same old days

Meet you at the cafe serving long-cold coffee
Talk into the grayness while the waitress fills your cup
I wish to be the heels under her surface
Forced into the linoleum with purpose

There's nothing here for me
In the checkered floors and dusty ceiling fans
My body's so much bigger than this booth
But we drone into the grayness
And we make plans.

Shower drain song as the remnants slip away
Leaving no sign that shampoo was there at all
The water turned cold 20 minutes ago
And I've let every needle fall

Meet my lipsticked mother at the bus stop
Home for a holiday that I forget
She holds me tight and talks of nothing
Ecstasy on two dead ears

There's nothing here for me
When their hands grab the last plate
I wasn't hungry anyway
I grew too old an hour ago

There's no one here for me
My bus ride back crawled by too fast
I gazed upon the empty bench
It's not my first, it's not my last

And every bench is built the same
I sat through sun and in the rain
I sit on steel and watch the train
Begging just to feel again.

# Fashion Trends These Days

Nicholas Jackson

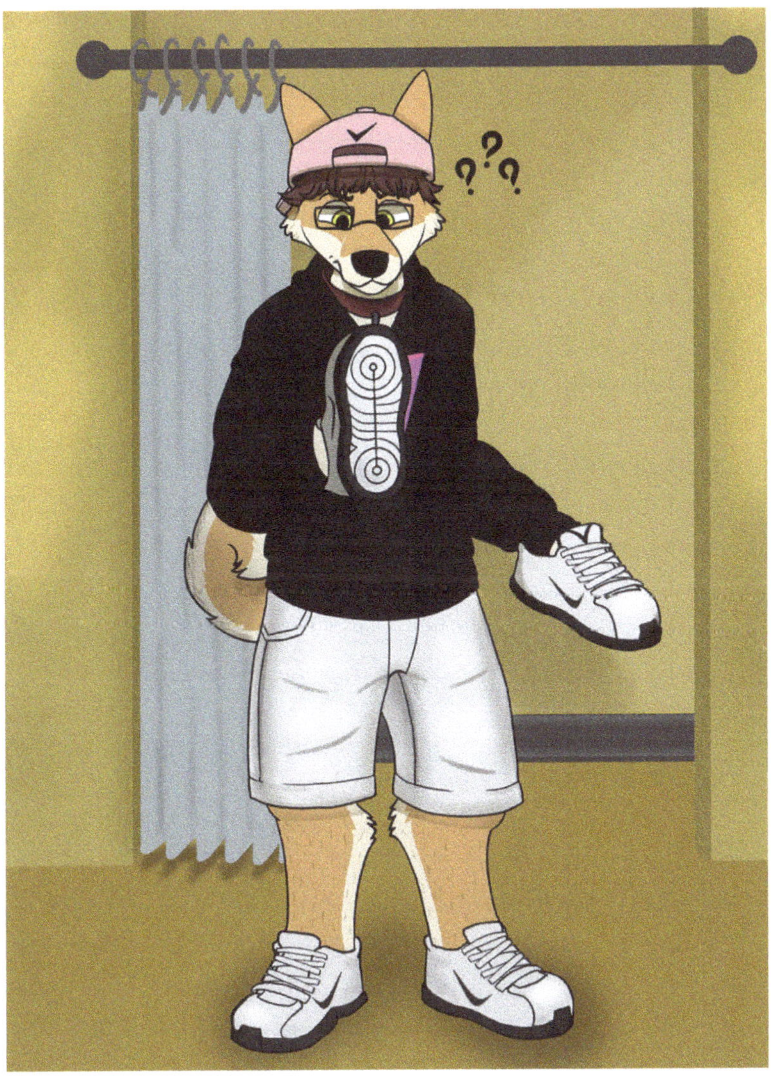

# You

## Destini Mink

Your face had always been as beautiful as it had been intimidating. Your dark hair had always framed your face in such a way, elongating your sharp and elegant cheekbones, contrasting with your strikingly pale blue eyes. Your cheeks were always dusted with the rosy pink from your favorite MAC Cosmetics blush that you kept in your Kohl's handbag, shade mauve.

I remember the day that we bought that handbag. We walked up and down the cluttered and overwhelmingly unfashionable aisles of the Kohl's purse rack together, perusing to find the cheapest but also cutest handbag we could. Your tall frame always towered over me. Like an ostrich towering over a canary or a robin. Like an ostrich, your shoulders sported a similar light but large feathery shawl. The color of the shawl matched your hair almost perfectly, and it seemed as though the two melted into one another as I followed you and watched you strut and swivel in the sea of faux leather and leopard print. You went with the delicate faux leather lavender clutch hanging by a long silver chain. It was impractically tiny, but fashionably a necessity. You jerked your head roughly to the side as another shopper neared us, and she walked away as quickly as she had come. I was always in awe of you. Your confidence to wear what you wished and to do as you pleased. Your power and ability to utilize your beauty as a weapon.

Your face with its perfect porcelain skin and straight pearly teeth. You smiled at me from across the table at lunch. We deserved a break from shopping. You looked so elegant even when you were devouring the greasy, drippy mess that was a Whopper with extra cheese and pickles and no ketchup.

Ketchup stains too drastically to eat in public. You never paid for extra cheese. Your smile always seemed to do that for you. The foolish and flabbergasted employee would always swallow hard and nod as they manually rang in your extra cheese for free when you asked so kindly, so sweetly, and with your perfect smile. Your ruby lipstick stayed perfectly in place as you practically unhinged your jaw to sink your perfect teeth into another bite. It was almost scary how you kept yourself within composure and maintained beauty that was sure to make others envy you, even when you just chugged your Coke Zero down in three big gulps. You had never appeared more beautiful to me.

Why now does your face look so different to me? Perhaps it is because with you laying there with your eyes closed. I cannot see your cyan eyes contrast with your straight and sharp ebony locks. Maybe you appear so different to me because instead of you towering over me, now I'm the ostrich and you're the canary. Delicate and small. Or maybe it is because your makeup was done by the elderly lady standing in the corner of the room, a black cardigan around her shoulders, trying to be as unnoticeable as possible. You would sneer in disgust at the pitiful wool that was draped around her shoulders. She dusted your cheeks with deep red rather than your favorite mauve. I would've remembered that. At least they gave you your bag. Your favorite bag. It was the only part of you lying before me that actually looked like you. You were gone.

# Sylvia Plath and Mathematics Worksheets

J.W. Surface

At the flat top podium
Bordered with worksheets.
In the comfort of my classroom,
With Sylvia between my hands
And butterflies—
Or rather,
Maniac bees—
In my stomach.
Surrounded by young minds
Eating up the poetry
Like the cookies I baked them.
And yet,
Among these minds
And worksheets,
There is no room.
There is no equation-filled board.
No cookies
For this after school club.
No eager eyes upon me.
No...
In this moment there is just
Sylvia
And I.
And her hard
And her firm
Words.
The boldness of her voice
Speaks through me,
Guiding me along her syllables,

Insistent
That respect be given
To her bees,
To her work,
To her.

# Memory Pockets

## Alec Cizak

You wear your memory
like perfect-fitting slacks.
And like any good pants,
pockets rest high on the side,
little caverns you can stuff
your hands into and let
your fingers walk around.

Sometimes, your pinky
brushes against a memory,
drinks the texture of a moment
you no longer control.

The first time
you kissed a girl
and meant it;
The first time you
stood up to
unreasonable authority
and paid the price;
The first time you
fled from a place of love
so scary, so unusual,
you didn't recognize
yourself.

Your thumb and middle finger
snap snap snap to pull you from
the dream of second chances
while your ring finger traces
torn seams and reminds you
it is naked.

# Train Car Archivists

## Mackenzie Hyatt

*Don't worry, it's the short train,*
coughed a bus stop mistress,
a status like mine,

with her tobacco-laced Hoosier articulation,
an accent falling out of fashion, it seems,
replaced by whatever feels fitting.

Apparently, she used to work for the trains,
just like some long-dead relative of mine

with one of the many titles
of my father's lineage
and thus of my own.

The engine scream,
what a century ago would be a coal-powered whistle,
rattled my ribcage all the same.

The concrete platform under my toes
shook in a way Indiana ground
wasn't supposed to.

(At least not before Indiana was what this ground was called.)

But the steel behemoth I expected
suddenly became a gallery,
and the prism of industry was shone through with a beam of
light.

Every color possible compressed, though sun-bleached,
in a can of spray paint
spelled words and names and portraits in loopy, bubbly
    lettering,

and all I can do is wonder
how the urbanite Van Goghs
found their way to their canvases

and how it doesn't matter to them if it's
Van Gogh like van Cough
or Van Gogh like van Go

only whether or not they can climb back over the train station
    fence
or keep pace with the crawling speed, slowly getting faster
    and more out of reach

and it dawned on me that whoever complains about
(and underpays people to scrub)
the aerosol calligraphy
really doesn't hate the art nor those creating it,

but instead despises the debate against their false idea
that anything public is anyone's property,
and can never be

someone's canvas.

# Yellow Mountain

Karen L. Newman

As the chill of winter began to lift and the Chinese national holiday approached, my Polish colleague, Maria, and I decided it was finally time for a trip to Yellow Mountain, the fabled pilgrimage spot in neighboring Anhui Province, where artists of past centuries went for inspiration to create the iconic scroll paintings one typically associates with classical Chinese painting—the craggy peaks shrouded in mist and lone pine trees clinging tenuously to the sides of sheer cliff faces.

Maria and I were both determined to have the most authentic experiences we possibly could in China, so we agreed that, rather than spending money for a ticket on a luxurious, high-speed train to our destination or booking a comfortable hotel room, we would instead hitchhike to Yellow Mountain and camp in the thirty-dollar tent I'd recently purchased at Ningbo's Decathlon megastore, where China's up-and-coming middle classes were outfitting themselves to partake in the newly-discovered joys of outdoor leisure and adventure activities that had been denied to them until the recent past.

On our appointed travel day, I waited for Maria downstairs near the entrance area of our apartment building, in between an abandoned couch, discarded clothing and household equipment, and pieces of broken metal—the general detritus of urban living that perpetually littered the landscape of our neighborhood. With backpacks in tow and snacks and drinks to tide us over for the unknowns of the day's trip that lay ahead, we planned our strategy. One of us had fashioned a makeshift sign from the flap of a cardboard box bearing the Chinese characters "Huang Shan," or Yellow Mountain, and with the sign to herald our destination, we felt ready for whatever adventure the fates might have in store for us that day. We first made a quick stop at our neighborhood fruit stand—a one-room shop run by a family consisting of mother, father, son, and grandfather, who all cooked and slept in a makeshift room at the back of the store—to stock up on a few tangerines and bananas for the trip. Maria had received directions from a Chinese colleague about the best spot to hitchhike from in town, namely, the entrance ramp to a highway toll plaza where we could most likely catch a ride from someone heading northwest, so we flagged down a taxi and directed the driver to deposit us there. After disembarking from the taxi and walking for a block or two, we realized that something wasn't quite right; despite the GPS maps our phones displayed to us, we couldn't locate the toll plaza that should have been right there in front of us. We walked back and forth and determined that—as was so common in a country single-mindedly driven to reinvent itself and lift itself from the muck of five millennia of rice paddies, a country that constructed new buildings and roads seemingly overnight—the toll-plaza had been closed, the entrance ramp blocked off, and the highway rerouted. There was no way for us to find a ride here, and so, since we were close to a line on Ningbo's sparkling, new subway system, we decided to take a train to one of its last terminals on the edge of town, where we knew a few newly constructed highways to converge.

As the warmth of the day descended upon us, Maria and I found ourselves standing on a road frequented by long-distance truckers, and we waved our cardboard sign with the large, black characters at passing vehicles. Soon enough, our enthusiasm began to wane as drivers gave us two foreign women puzzled looks, or waved, or sped on without giving us a second thought.

A trucker and his wife, who clung to his arm in the front seat of their cab and who both appeared to be from the mountainous regions of southern China, stared intently at us as they motored past, multiple good luck charms hanging from their rear-view mirror to sanctify their homeward journey of two thousand miles or more. Nobody stopped, save for a young man on a scooter who stared intently at us and asked us what we were doing, as if it weren't patently obvious. Perhaps he wished he could tear himself away from the obligations of big-city life like we were about to; perhaps he just couldn't stop gazing at the novelty of two strange, vagabond women standing on the side of the road with backpacks, a bundled tent, and a homemade sign.

As the minutes turned into an hour, then two, we soon realized that this hitchhiking locale would be fruitless, so we returned to our own district of town where I knew for certain a busy a toll plaza to be, as it was the toll plaza my driver took each time I arrived in Ningbo for the semester and returned to four months later, when it was time for me to depart again for the Shanghai airport. Back Maria and I went, by subway train and bus, and three hours later we found ourselves standing about a mile and a half from where we had initially begun our journey. Dispirited, we lingered at the highway entrance ramp, half-heartedly waving our sign, and within minutes of our arrival, it began to rain. We hurriedly raised our umbrellas, the ever-present protection we carried against the ubiquitous, pop-up springtime rainstorms, and just as we were about to ask ourselves if it was really worth it to stand in what might soon become a deluge—in the middle of a Chinese megacity, on a highway entrance ramp, looking to hitch a ride with a homemade cardboard sign whose ink was starting to run—a newer-model BMW pulled over, and the young driver motioned us in, inviting us to join him on his two-hour journey to Hangzhou, which, while not our final aim, would at least get us halfway to our legendary destination.

# Yellow Mountain

Karen L. Newman

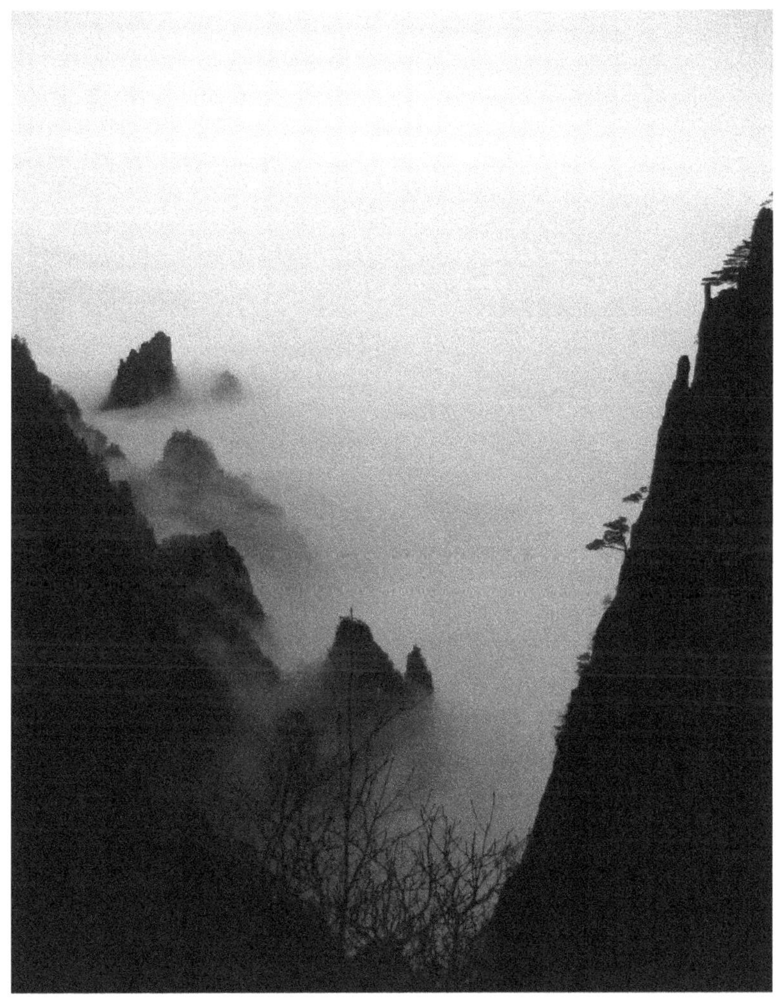

# Contributor Biographies

**Adam Fernandes** is a senior visual communication design student who loves experimentation and creativity. He hopes to work in a creative agency where he can come up with new ideas in graphic design and creative strategy for companies that are well integrated into people's lives. Adam could also play his guitar all day. He once got asked by a neighbor on his floor to turn down the volume of his guitar. That day, Adam truly felt like a rockstar. Not to mention, the neighbor liked the music, although it was a little loud for her taste.

**Alec Cizak** is a writer and filmmaker from Indiana. His latest novel, *Cool It Down,* is available from ABC Group Documentation. He is also the editor of the genre fiction and pop culture digest, *Pulp Modern.*

**Alex Phillips-Hedge** is a sophomore at the University of Indianapolis. In his free time, he enjoys listening to music to inspire random instances of creativity whether it is poetry, photography, or his own music. He is currently exploring what he actually wants to do with his life.

**Alrielle Viewegh** is a junior at the University of Indianapolis majoring in English and secondary education, minoring in creative writing, and has an honors concentration. She is also the design editor for *Etchings* 34.2, secretary for the Student Education Association, and one of the Assistants to the Writing Lab Director.

**Breanna Emmett** is a double major in creative writing and art. Creativity and imagination have always been core values of her life. Her greatest inspiration is her cat, Pippington "Pip", who inspires her to get out of bed and write by meowing at ungodly hours of the morning.

**Cambel Castle** is a freshman at the University of Indianapolis majoring in pre-art therapy with studio art. She enjoys creating art and writing poems. Her best works usually happen at night. She loves for her work to have a deeper meaning or represent a feeling or experience. Cambel always hopes for her viewer/reader to experience a connection or emotion with her piece.

**Cassi Dillon** is a senior English major at the University of Indianapolis.

**Desteni Guidry** is a junior at the University of Indianapolis majoring in English with a minor in creative writing. She is also the design editor for *Etchings* 34.2. In her free time, she enjoys listening to music, playing video games, and reading.

**Destini Mink** is a junior psychology and English creative writing major at the University of Indianapolis. She really loves to write and hopes to get her name out there.

**Elizabeth Dubak** is from Eminence, Indiana, and is currently a sophomore studying pre-art therapy at the University of Indianapolis. She enjoys working on art, including photography, painting, and drawing. She also enjoys reading and listening to music in her free time.

**Emma Knaack** is a sophomore professional writing and creative writing major minoring in business administration with an honors and teaching English language learners concentration at the University of Indianapolis. She is Etchings magazine's submissions editor for issue 34.2, editorial assistant for *Indy Her Campus*, and a member of Phi Alpha Epsilon. In her free time, she enjoys thrifting, reading manga, watching anime, and listening to Korean and Japanese music.

**Ethan Thurston** is a junior creative writing major.

**Grace Carrender** is a freshman studying secondary English education. She's a part of UIndy's Honors College and Student Education Association. In her free time, she enjoys creative writing, visiting book and antique stores, and playing with her dog, Tayla.

**Hannah Biedess** is a sophomore at the University of Indianapolis. She is double majoring in professional and creative writing.

**J. W. Surface** emerged from the University of Indianapolis in 2013. Currently, he teaches mathematics to brilliant high school students during the day and writes poetry and fiction at night. He is indebted to God for blessing him with these two rewarding passions, and to his wife for putting up with his consistent, strange nonsense. His poetry has appeared in *Etchings* Magazine. You can follow him on Goodreads.com.

**Jonathan Thang** is a senior at the University of Indianapolis. He has no prior published works. If you were to ask him whether he believes he has a future in writing, he would respond by asking whether he has a future at all. He recently purchased a new pair of shoes—women's because all the men's were too large for him.

**Jordan Dashiell** is a sophomore at the University of Indianapolis studying social work. Originally planning to go to school for songwriting, Jordan has been writing his own music since he was fifteen and wrote poetry as soon as he was old enough to pick up a pencil. The main emotions expressed in his writings are sadness, longing, and numbness, as they are the most poignant and fascinating to him. In his free time, Jordan likes to lay in bed and debate whether or not he should get up.

**Kaitlyn McCoy** is in her second year of being an English literature and secondary education major at the University of Indianapolis, as well as being a student-athlete on the Swimming and Diving team. She's originally from Phoenix, Arizona.

**Karen L. Newman** is an Associate Professor in the English Department at the University of Indianapolis, where she offers courses in teaching English as a second language (TESOL), composition, literature, modern arts, and service learning. Her research interests include teacher professional development and international education. An avid world traveler, she has lived abroad for more than twenty years and visited thirty-five countries. She serves on the Board of Women Writing for (a) Change - Bloomington and enjoys the healing powers of the arts, especially writing creative nonfiction and experimenting with ceramics and photography.

**Liza Harris** is a junior majoring in English creative writing. She is from Illinois and hopes to be a manuscript editor like her favorite character, Margaret Tate, from *The Proposal.* When she is not in classes or doing homework, she spends time writing poetry and fictional works.

**Mackenzie Hyatt** is a senior at the University of Indianapolis and is majoring in four-field anthropology. Her favorite book is *A Thousand Splendid Suns* by Khaled Hosseini, and she wishes she could sit still long enough to read *War & Peace.* She would like to remind you that you are loved.

**Mia Lehmkuhl** is a freshman at the University of Indianapolis studying entrepreneurship and finance. She has been writing since elementary school and has fallen in love with poetry and storytelling. She writes poetry in times of adversity and in times of great happiness, and she loves to share her work as those who inspired her once did so that perhaps she could have the same effect on another.

**Nicholas Jackson** is a sophomore at the University of Indianapolis. He is currently studying studio art and going for a concentration in animation and illustration.

**Olivia Cameron** is a sophomore creative writing and professional writing major. She enjoys writing fiction that primarily focuses on women and psychological horror. Her goal is to be a creative writing professor and published author.

**Sam Jackson** is a senior English major, with a focus in creative writing and a minor in professional writing. Outside of the classroom, he enjoys writing poetry and hopes to make a career out of that someday. This is his first time having his work published in a literary magazine!

**Shyam Patel** is studying computer science at the University of Indianapolis. He is not a good writer by any means but tries his best. Some of Shyam's hobbies are listening to music, working out, hiking, and dancing. He likes a nice warm cup of tea and good poetry before going to bed. His writings could be from his feelings at that time or fictional, but, mostly, they are fictional.

**Sierra Durbin** is a sophomore majoring in creative writing and minoring in music at the University of Indianapolis. She performs in three choirs at the school, including the Greyhound Sound Show Choir. Sierra is a writer and graphic designer at *Her Campus* at Indy and a writer, actor, and social media manager in UIndy Film Club. Besides singing and writing being her major passions in life, she loves fashion, dance, and photography. Some of her work has been published in *Etchings*, and she is currently working on publishing more and becoming an influencer and internet performer under the name, "Sierrallstar."

**Sydney Pinkstaff** is a sophomore at the University of Indianapolis majoring in pre-art therapy and minoring in photography. Sydney enjoys painting, photography, and going outside of the box with her art. In her free time, she enjoys making art and going on walks with her dog, Auggie.

**Sydney Smith** is a freshman at the University of Indianapolis majoring in communications with an emphasis in electronic media. In her free time, Sydney loves to travel and take photos, and she aspires to show others the beauty of the little things in her work.

**Z Wilkinson** is a creative writing major and professional writing minor at the University of Indianapolis. He hopes to write and edit works exploring mental health, disability, and LGBTQIA+ issues. He enjoys creating character-based digital artwork and playing video games in his free time.

# Colophon

Interior text is set in the Bell MT font family.
The cover font is in Bernard MT Condensed and Perpetua.

# Call for Submissions

***Etchings Magazine* Volume 35 Issue 1, Fall 2022**
**Submissions due at 11:55 pm EST on September 12, 2022.**

Guidelines for Submission:

• All UIndy students, faculty, staff, and alumni are invited to submit.

• All accepted undergraduate prose and poetry submissions will be considered for the Dorlis Gott Armentrout Award.

• Up to three short stories or creative nonfiction essays, five poems, five visual materials, and five audio files may be submitted.

• Visual submissions: for best print results, consider the 5.5 x 8 portrait page with .25 margins and flatten files to 300 ppi *.tiff CMYK 8 bit files.

• Poetry and Prose: present poems as single-spaced and prose double-spaced with both formatted in Microsoft Word (.doc, .docx, or .odt) in a 12-point font.

• Audio: submit .mp3 files, and present scores/lyrics following the guidelines for visual or poetry submissions above.

• *Etchings Magazine* has a blind submission process, so please do not include any personal identifiers in your submission files (this information will be provided through Submittable when you submit your work).

Learn more about Etchings Press at etchings.uindy.edu
Submit work at etchings.submittable.com.
We do not accept email submissions. Please create a free account at submittable.com or sign in using Facebook.
For questions, email us at etchings@uindy.edu
Follow us @uindyetchings on the platforms below:

www.ingramcontent.com/pod-product-compliance
Lightning Source LLC
Chambersburg PA
CBHW050036040726
47599CB00015B/1711

* 9 7 8 1 9 5 5 5 2 1 0 4 8 *